To

From

Date

PRAYERS
to Soothe Your Soul

Artwork by
Sandy Lynam Clough
Original Prayers by **Hope Lyda**

H®
HARVEST HOUSE PUBLISHERS

EUGENE, OREGON

Design and production by Garborg Design Works, Savage, Minnesota

PRAYERS TO SOOTHE YOUR SOUL
Copyright © 2010 by Harvest House Publishers
Published by Harvest House Publishers
Eugene, Oregon 97402
www.harvesthousepublishers.com
ISBN 978-0-7369-2780-2

Contents

The prayer that begins with thankfulness, and passes on into waiting, even while in sorrow and sore need, will always end in thankfulness, and triumph, and praise.

ALEXANDER MACLAREN

Encouragement

But you are a shield around me, O LORD; you
bestow glory on me and lift up my head.
To the LORD I cry aloud, and he answers me
from his holy hill.

Selah

I lie down and sleep; I wake again, because
the LORD sustains me.

PSALM 3:3-5

4

Wondrous is the strength of cheerfulness, and its power of endurance—the cheerful man will do more in the same time, will do it better, will preserve it longer, than the sad or sullen.

THOMAS CARLYLE

God, I have praised You, and I have lifted up words of gratitude over the years. I know You are with me at all times. Now, I cry out to You as my heart aches. With each groan, I feel the response of Your sustaining love. Your protection and presence show me that there is hope for today and joy for my tomorrow. Amen.

5

Kind words are the

REV. FREDERICK WILLIAM FABER

Lord, I hear the melody of hope and gladness. It comes to me as I sit waiting for peace and comfort. Immediately, my restlessness is replaced with tranquility. I am kept from harm in the hiding place of Your grace. The song that fills my being becomes a wellspring of gladness. Only You can turn the desert of my trial into a place of nourishment and celebration. Amen.

music of the world.

You are my
hiding place;
you will protect
me from trouble
and surround
me with songs
of deliverance.

PSALM 32:7

In the desert a fountain is springing,
In the wide waste there still is a tree,
And a bird in the solitude singing,
Which speaks to my spirit of thee.

LORD BYRON

Encouragement

7

Beauty

One thing I ask of the LORD, this is what I seek:
that I may dwell in the house of the LORD
all the days of my life, to gaze upon the beauty of the LORD
and to seek him in his temple.

PSALM 27:4

Flowers are God's thoughts of beauty taking
form to gladden mortal gaze; bright gems
of earth, in which, perchance, we see
what Eden was—what Paradise may be!

WILLIAM WILBERFORCE

*God, when I hunger for solace and
protection, I seek the covering of
Your care. There is such sweetness in
the house of the Lord. You usher me
in with open arms. Your embrace fills
my heart with relief and joy, and
I am transformed by the beauty of
unconditional love. Amen.*

well drained
soil

Beauty

He has caused his wonders to be remembered; the LORD is gracious and compassionate.

PSALM 111:4

I pray thee, O God,

10

Lord, open my eyes to witness the intricate design of nature, the remarkable wonder of the majestic moon in the night sky and the brilliance of another sunrise. These exquisite gifts from Your hand to this world provide deep comfort and solace—they remind me of Your love of beauty and Your desire for Your children to know such beauty. Amen.

Never lose an opportunity of seeing anything beautiful, for beauty is God's handwriting.

RALPH WALDO EMERSON

that I may be beautiful within.

SOCRATES

11

Hope

I will praise you forever for what you
have done; in your name I will hope,
for your name is good.

PSALM 52:9

12

It is only through the morning gate of the beautiful that you can penetrate into the realm of knowledge. That which we feel here as beauty, we shall one day know as truth.

JOHANN CHRISTOPH FRIEDRICH VON SCHILLER

God, when I look at the delights of Your creation, I experience a rush of hope and gratitude. The birds who soar on colorful wings above and the brilliant, delicate flowers that line the pathway are gifts of beauty and evidence of Your care. I praise You for the opportunity to experience Your artistry and abundance in this lifetime. Amen.

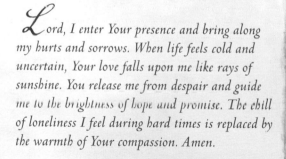

May your unfailing love
rest upon us, O LORD, even
as we put our hope in you.

PSALM 33:22

*Lord, I enter Your presence and bring along
my hurts and sorrows. When life feels cold and
uncertain, Your love falls upon me like rays of
sunshine. You release me from despair and guide
me to the brightness of hope and promise. The chill
of loneliness I feel during hard times is replaced by
the warmth of Your compassion. Amen.*

14

Our prayer and God's mercy are
like two buckets in a well; while
the one ascends, the other descends.

MARK HOPKINS

Comfort

You will restore my life again; from the depths of the earth you will again bring me up. You will increase my honor and comfort me once again.

PSALM 71:20-21

What a proof of the Divine tenderness is there in the human heart itself, which is the organ and receptacle of so many sympathies! When we consider how exquisite are those conditions by which it is even made capable of so much suffering—the capabilities of a child's heart, of a mother's heart—what must be the nature of Him who fashioned its depths, and strung its chords?

EDWIN HUBBELL CHAPIN

Lord, I know Your presence to be real. This knowledge carries me today as I face an obstacle that troubles me. I have been broken. I have been weary. And You have been faithful during my most difficult journeys. With great gratitude, I praise You today for the wholeness, the awakening, and the comfort that will come from Your care. Amen.

When anxiety was great within me, your consolation brought joy to my soul.

Comforter and Lord, I rest in Your care today. People around me aren't sure what to say or how to ease my trouble. While their presence and kindness offers a sense of physical support, it is Your presence that is a balm for my spiritual hurts. You soothe my soul with eternal assurances and glimpses of joy. I am consoled in the protective nest of Your heart. Amen.

18

I have enjoyed many of the comforts of life, none of which I wish to esteem lightly; yet I confess I know not any joy that is so dear to me, that so fully satisfies the inmost desires of my mind, that so enlivens, refines, and elevates my whole nature, as that which I derive from religion—from faith in God. May this God be thy God, thy refuge, thy comfort, as he has been mine.

JOHANN KASPAR LAVATER

19

Hope is like the wing of an angel, soaring up to heaven, and bearing our prayers to the throne of God.

Jeremy Taylor

Promises

My comfort in my suffering is this: Your promise preserves my life.

Psalm 119:50

Lord, You lift me up when loss weighs me down spiritually, physically, and emotionally. There is comfort in Your eternal view of life. My longing for restoration is my longing to be in more meaningful communion with You. These troubles will not sway me from Your presence but will lead me to the hope of Your promises. Amen.

Our sweetest experiences of affection are meant to point us to that realm which is the real and endless home of the heart.

HENRY WARD BEECHER

Oh, Lord, my steps falter, and I struggle to remain upright under the weight of my need. I am grateful for listening friends and concerned family members, but when night falls, I sit alone with my cares. In the silence, I give to You my frailties and move forward in Your strength. Your promises are my stepping stones. And should I fall, You will catch me and set me in the direction of hope. Amen.

The greatest attribute

Promises

Cast your cares
on the LORD
and he will
sustain you; he
will never let the
righteous fall.

PSALM 55:22

The steps of faith fall on the seeming
void, but find the rock beneath.

JOHN GREENLEAF WHITTIER

of heaven is mercy.

FRANCIS BEAUMONT

23

Grace

In the morning, O LORD, you
hear my voice; in the morning
I lay my requests before you
and wait in expectation.

PSALM 5:3

*Happiness is
neither within
us only, or
without us;
it is the union
of ourselves
with God.*

BLAISE PASCAL

God, when I rise in the morning, Your tender grace is shining before me. I don't have to search the horizon to find You because You are with me always. My prayers can be whispers, shouts, or silent petitions that radiate from my heart. You recognize my soul's cry because You created me. With mercy, You hear Your child's prayer. Amen.

Oh, God, how beautiful the thought, how merciful the blest decree, that grace can always be found when sought, and nought shut out the soul from thee.

ELIZA COOK

Grace

25

The LORD is gracious and righteous;
our God is full of compassion.
The LORD protects the simplehearted;
when I was in great need, he saved me.

PSALM 116:5-6

26

Walk in the light and thou shalt see thy
   path, though thorny, bright;
for God, by grace, shall dwell in thee,
   and God himself is light.

*Lord, Your love lights the way for me to walk
this journey. You are my consistent beacon along the
unsteady terrain. Thank You for always receiving
my simple prayers and for discerning the hidden
needs of my heart. You never turn me away; instead,
You beckon me to dwell beneath the canopy of Your
compassion. I am saved by Your limitless grace. Amen.*

Renewal

Praise the LORD, O my soul, and forget not all his
benefits—who forgives all your sins and heals all
your diseases, who redeems your life from the pit
and crowns you with love and compassion,
who satisfies your desires with good things so that
your youth is renewed like the eagle's.

PSALM 103:2-5

*A human heart can never grow old if it takes a lively
interest in the pairing of birds, the reproduction of
flowers, and the changing tints of autumn leaves.*

LYDIA MARIA CHILD

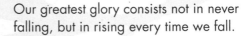

Our greatest glory consists not in never falling, but in rising every time we fall.

OLIVER GOLDSMITH

Lord, sometimes troubles loom so large in my mind that I lose sight of the desires in my heart. In Your gracious way, You redeem me from despair and restore to me a sense of joy. Through the goodness of friends, the intimacy of prayer, and the daily evidence of Your provision, my desires for goodness are renewed. Amen.

29

Renewal

God, the covering of Your mercy is so gentle. Nothing soothes my soul like Your loving-kindness. I hold out my hands each day to receive Your blessing and wisdom. I start with nothing, and You replenish my reserves and show me the bounty of faith. I'm in awe that in my time of need, I am also experiencing a time of plenty. You amaze me, Lord. Amen.

But I have trusted in Your lovingkindness;
My heart shall rejoice in Your salvation.
I will sing to the LORD,
Because He has dealt bountifully with me.

PSALM 13:5-6 NASB

Mercy among the virtues
is like the moon among the
stars—not so sparkling and
vivid as many, but dispensing
a calm radiance that hallows
the whole. It is the bow that
rests upon the bosom of the
cloud when the storm is past.

E.H. CHAPIN

31

Whatever enlarges hope

Trust

Commit your way to the LORD;
trust in him and he will do this: He
will make your
righteousness shine
like the dawn, the
justice of your cause
like the noonday sun.

PSALM 37:5-6

will also exalt courage.

WILLIAM SAMUEL JOHNSON

All I have seen teaches
me to trust the creator
for all I have not seen.

RALPH WALDO EMERSON

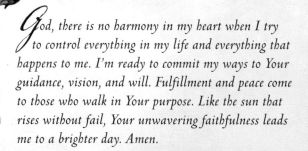

*God, there is no harmony in my heart when I try
to control everything in my life and everything that
happens to me. I'm ready to commit my ways to Your
guidance, vision, and will. Fulfillment and peace come
to those who walk in Your purpose. Like the sun that
rises without fail, Your unwavering faithfulness leads
me to a brighter day. Amen.*

33

I trust in God's unfailing love for ever and ever. I will praise you forever for what you have done; in your name I will hope, for your name is good.

PSALM 52:8-9

Lord, I behold the tiniest seed and the tallest tree with awe. You conceived these just as You shaped heaven, earth, eternity, and me. I praise Your name for all You have done and all that You will do. And I call upon Your name with complete trust for my every need because You created me to be a part of this eternal thread of miracles. Amen.

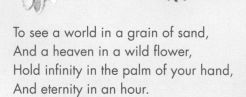

Trust

Life is before you; not an earthly life alone,
but an endless life; a thread running
interminably through the work of eternity.

J.G. HOLLAND

To see a world in a grain of sand,
And a heaven in a wild flower,
Hold infinity in the palm of your hand,
And eternity in an hour.

WILLIAM BLAKE

Peace

Many are asking, "Who can show us any good?"
Let the light of your face shine upon us, O LORD.
You have filled my heart with greater joy
than when their grain and new wine abound.
I will lie down and sleep in peace,
for you alone, O LORD, make me dwell in safety.

PSALM 4:6-8

Lord, there is so much to be grateful for every day. The difficulties and sorrows I face do not challenge my understanding of Your compassion; they offer me more intimate encounters with it. When others search high and low for evidence of goodness in this life, I can point to You with confidence as the way of peace and contentment. You alone fulfill me and satisfy my soul. Amen.

The best and sweetest flowers in paradise, God gives to his people when they are on their knees in the closet. Prayer, if not the very gate of heaven, is the key to let us into its holiness and joys.

THOMAS BROOKS

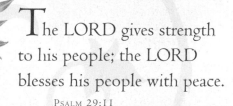

The LORD gives strength to his people; the LORD blesses his people with peace.

PSALM 29:11

God, there are many people around me who are longing for the tangibles of blessing and strength. They want the abundance of wealth and the earthly assurances of possession and success. But I know that my peace comes with Your provision alone. The abundance of spiritual truth, the riches of faith, the bounty of belief—these are the treasures of my peace in You. Amen.

Peace does not dwell in outward things,
but within the soul; we may preserve it in
the midst of the bitterest pain, if our will
remain firm and submissive. Peace in this
life springs from acquiescence, not in an
exemption from suffering.

FRANCOIS FÉNELON

Peace

Refuge and Strength

God is our refuge and strength, an ever-present help in trouble. Therefore we will not fear, though the earth give way and the mountains fall into the heart of the sea, though its waters roar and foam and the mountains quake with their surging.

PSALM 46:1-3

Where mercy, love, and pity

Lord, the big world of nations, wars, famine, and natural disasters is overwhelming. But even my smaller world of daily tasks, health and financial concerns, and the ongoing needs of my family is more than I can bear. You don't remove me from these worlds, You call me to trust the refuge of Your divine care. Troubles befall Your children, but they are always met with the rise of Your grace and faithfulness. Amen.

...well, there God is dwelling too.

WILLIAM BLAKE

41

Lord, You hold me in the palm of Your hand. I can be there during the rush of traffic or the stillness of a restless night. The weight of my body, burdens, and to-do list feel like a feather in Your outstretched, mighty hand. You don't ask me to journey to Your refuge. Your sanctuary and strength are my starting place. From here my heart can follow wherever You lead. Amen.

Just as there comes a warm sunbeam into every cottage window, so comes a love-beam of God's care and pity for every separate need.

NATHANIEL HAWTHORNE

He who dwells in the shelter of the Most High
will rest in the shadow of the Almighty.
I will say of the LORD, "He is my refuge
and my fortress, my God, in whom I trust."

PSALM 91:1-2

43

Faith

Love and faithfulness meet together;
righteousness and peace kiss each other.
Faithfulness springs forth from the earth,
and righteousness looks down from heaven.
The LORD will indeed give what is good,
and our land will yield its harvest.

PSALM 85:10-12

Every tomorrow
has two handles.
We can take
hold of it with
the handle of
anxiety or the
handle of faith.

HENRY WARD BEECHER

*Provider and Lord, how I rest in the knowledge that
what You give to me is good and right for this time. You
show me the wonder of Your provision and faithfulness.
I will take in these assurances now, and I will watch
for a future harvest with anticipation. Faith leads me
to peace even when I don't know what tomorrow will
bring. Amen.*

45

Trust in him at all times, O people; pour out your hearts to him, for God is our refuge.

PSALM 62:8

Lord, the concerns come tumbling from my lips. I know that You hear them and care about each and every one of them. I entrust You with my innermost thoughts, fears, and hopes. I step into the safety of Your refuge with immense gratitude and relief. You are my resting place. Your faithfulness is my greatest comfort. Amen.

Faith

Every good and
holy desire,
though it lack the form, hath,
notwithstanding, in itself the
substance, and with God the
force of prayer; Who regardeth
the very moanings, groans, and
sighs of the heart of man.

THOMAS HOOKER

Love

est me, O LORD, and try me,
examine my heart and my mind; for
your love is ever before me, and I
walk continually in your truth.

PSALM 26:2-3

*For everything
that lives is holy,
life delights in life.*

WILLIAM BLAKE

48

Love

Life is made up, not of great sacrifices or duties, but of little things, in which smiles and kindnesses, and small obligations given habitually, are what preserve the heart and secure comfort.

SIR H. DAVY

Lord, have I been faithful in the little things? Do I extend kindnesses that are genuine? Do I encourage the best in Your children? Give me Your vision so that I may witness the big and small opportunities to be generous. May I let Your love flow freely to others without judgment, ego, or fear so that compassion and goodness are my journey companions. Amen.

49

To love and be loved is the

They were glad when it grew calm, and he guided them to their desired haven. Let them give thanks to the LORD for his unfailing love and his wonderful deeds for men.

PSALM 107:30-31

There is in life no blessing like affection; it soothes, it hallows, elevates, subdues, and bringeth down to earth its native heaven: life has nought else that may supply its place.

L.E. LANDON

greatest happiness of existence.

SYDNEY SMITH

*God, when I am afraid,
You usher me to safety and
prepare a place for me to rest
my mind and spirit. In the
haven of Your care, Your
calming presence assures me
that Your purpose prevails
over my failings, mistakes,
and worries. Your love is my
protection and is a salve to
my fears. It is my greatest
blessing. Amen.*

51

Rest

Find rest, O my soul, in God alone;
my hope comes from him.
He alone is my rock and my salvation;
he is my fortress, I will not be shaken.

God, there is rest for the restless. In You I discover a hope that refreshes and transforms. I have stood on the shifting sands of the world's false promises, and I have watched my version of success erode away. What remains is the certainty of Your will and purpose. Without hesitation, I place my trust in You, and I rest in Your unshakable promises. Amen.

How often we look upon God as our last and feeblest resource! We go to him because we have nowhere else to go. And then we learn that the storms of life have driven us, not upon the rocks, but into the desired haven.

GEORGE MACDONALD

Meditation is the soul's perspective glass, whereby, in her long removes, she discerneth God, as if he were nearer at hand.

OWEN FELTHAM

Restore to me the joy of your salvation and grant me a willing spirit, to sustain me.

PSALM 51:12

Lord, I have expended too much energy trying to save myself. My days are more wisely spent meditating on the joy and blessings that flow from Your salvation. When I tread the rocky waters of worry, Your strength preserves me and pulls me to the safety of love's shore. I lean into Your grace, restored once more. Amen.

The heart that is to be filled to the brim with holy joy must be held still.

GEORGE SEATON BOWES

55

Compassion

Turn to me and be gracious to me,
for I am lonely and afflicted.

PSALM 25:16

*Lord, during this time of sadness,
You see right through my attempts to
be strong. You see that I am broken and
in great need of Your compassion. You
ease the pain that rises
up within me. I am no longer
lonely, because I feel the power
of Your presence, and Your
unconditional love transforms my
sorrow into blessing. Amen.*

Said a wise man to one in deep sorrow, "I did not come to comfort you; God only can do that; but I did come to say how deeply and tenderly I feel for you in your affliction."

TRYON EDWARDS

There is a ministry of "presence." The fact that you are there with the one who is suffering can often help more than any words you say.

SANDY LYNAM CLOUGH

Mmay your unfailing love be my comfort,
according to your promise to your servant.
Let your compassion come to me that I may live,
for your law is my delight.

PSALM 119:76-77

In all ranks of
life the human heart
yearns for the beautiful;
and the beautiful things
that God makes are his
gift to all alike.

HARRIET BEECHER STOWE

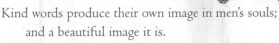

ssion

Kind words produce their own image in men's souls;
    and a beautiful image it is.
They soothe and quiet and comfort the hearer.

BLAISE PASCAL

Lord, the way to a whole and meaningful life is discovered in the garden of Your mercy. As I walk with You there, You speak words of comfort into my soul, and I am renewed. During this season of life, I have longed for beauty and kindness, and I find them in abundance through Your compassion. Thank You for loving me. Amen.

Joy

Y ou, O LORD, keep my lamp burning;
my God turns my darkness into light.

PSALM 18:28

There is sweet joy that

Lord, during a trial, clouds of uncertainty or disbelief can cover my eyes and my heart. I avoid the brightness of contentment because I am afraid to be let down. But You eliminate the darkness with the light of possibility. Joy is behind those clouds! Oh how Your love illuminates comfort and peace when I am willing to see, follow, and believe. Amen.

Great joy, especially after a sudden change of circumstances, is apt to be silent, and dwells rather in the heart than on the tongue.

HENRY FIELDING

comes to us through sorrow.

CHARLES SPURGEON

I will praise you, O LORD, with all my heart;
I will tell of all your wonders.
I will be glad and rejoice in you;
I will sing praise to your name, O Most High.

PSALM 9:1-2

O Most High, I lift up my eyes, my hands, and my words to praise You. Every season of life is filled with reminders of Your tenderness and affection. You soften my heart when I am tempted to close it off to the world. You breathe new life into my days when I need refreshment. I celebrate the miracles of Your love and restoration. Amen.

JOY

Happiness is like manna; it is to be gathered in grains, and enjoyed every day. It will not keep; it cannot be accumulated; nor have we got to go out of ourselves or into remote places to gather it since it is rained down from Heaven, at our very doors.

TYRON EDWARDS

63